Foreword

Pulling together over 60 years of recruitment experience, we have compiled what we believe is a highly practical and easy to follow job hunting and CV writing guide for those looking to work in the United Kingdom or Republic of Ireland.

Having helped several thousand job seekers achieve employment across the UK and Ireland, we have taken key elements of our advice and detailed them in this guide.

The guide is a step-by-step, teach yourself instruction manual.

Recruiters may spend as little as 15 seconds when first appraising a CV; in the case of a teenager's CV, a survey in The Times states this is 8.8 seconds. This means making a quick and immediate impact is essential. This guide will show you how.

Included within the CV writing section are CV templates and advice on how to apply our CV writing techniques at all levels and across all disciplines.

For those looking for entry level positions, we cover: apprenticeship CVs; school leaver CVs; and graduate CVs.

We will also show you how to write a CV if you are looking for a change of career and transferable skill-based functional CVs.

Job hunting techniques have also changed radically in the last 10 years and our experience tells us that many people do not use all the job search tools available, or do not use them to the fullest. We cover areas including: the meta-crawlers; CV databases; social media and the use of LinkedIn. We help you to build a focused action plan whilst ensuring you maximise your activity.

Highly practical in nature, this is a guide you will keep in a safe place 'just in case'.

JOBS .3 DOC

Contents

CV writing

Before we look at how to structure a CV, you need to make sure you are creating the most visual impact. A poorly laid out CV will be interpreted by a recruiter as potential lack of ability, or even overlooked completely.

Optimise your CVs visual impact

An important point to note is that the top half of the CV is your 'shop window'; it is the first part of your CV viewed on a computer when opened. If in this area you don't start to highlight the skills the recruiter is looking for, or start to imply you are a potential candidate, will they read any further? So use this space well – having all the key facts hidden away on page 2 will do you no favours.

When writing a CV, many people try and stick to the '2-page rule': that a CV should not be more than 2 pages long. To fit 2 pages, they often shrink the font size and widen the margins. If you are not careful, this turns a CV into a 'wall of words' and makes it unappealing to read.

Interviewers also tend to interview candidates using paper copy CVs so make sure your CV is easy to read when printed by using a good-sized font.

As for the '2-page rule', in reality a 3-page CV is quite acceptable if full of relevant facts and not full of waffle. Page 3 is often where you list courses, training and your qualifications, so do not be afraid to use a 3-page CV.

For some people, such as IT contractors or individuals with a history of working on short term roles, 4 or 5-page CVs may be necessary as you detail the relevant facts.

Finally, to cater for those who are looking to find specific facts about you, make sure transitions within your CV are easy to follow by using spacing between sections and by enlarging the font or by the use of underlining or bold.

Basic CV writing tips

Other factors to consider are:

- Your most recent employer should be on page 1, going backwards in time
- Try not to use jargon, although industry jargon such as JIT is acceptable
- Include 'the numbers' such as 'managed a team of...' or 'responsible for a budget of...' – it is this detail that helps a recruiter measure your capabilities
- Education over 10 years old can be put at the end of your CV. For students, however, education should be on page 1
- Although qualifications should be placed at the end of your CV, if a qualification is relevant to your career, reference it on page 1 (covered later)
- Make your CV easy to read by using bullet points
- Choose a modern font to write your CV in

- Be careful with colour and using italic writing. If you do introduce colour, try printing your CV in black and white to see how it looks
- Spell-check your final CV / proofread at 150% normal size
- No need to include your date of birth, although for younger people we often include their age as it helps highlight that they are just starting out
- If sentences in a grammar check show up as grammatically incorrect (green wiggly line underneath) simply leave off the full stop on that line and the green wiggly line will disappear
- Make sure things line up vertically by using the tab spacer. Using the space bar will often resulting in non-perfect alignment = poor presentation
- Finally, with dashes, make sure they are all the same length

Remember, if the job requires high attention to detail and there are spelling errors, things badly aligned, or gaps and spaces where they should not appear, what does this say about your attention to detail?

The 15 second rule / focus your CV to the role

A typical mistake many people make is to write a CV to recount their life story and expect the recruiter to find what they are looking for in the CV. Many people we work with still think a recruiter will spend 3 or 4 minutes appraising a CV, however this is not the case.

With the introduction of online job hunting there has been an increase in the number of applicants and as a result the time recruiters take to screen a CV has dropped. To demonstrate how things have changed, in a 2015 survey in 'The Times' it was highlighted that recruiters appraise the average teenager's CV in 8.8 seconds. If over 19 years of age... this leaps to approximately 15 to 30 seconds.

In both cases we are talking about recruiters dealing with high volumes of applications, but that is, in effect, most recruiters working in HR departments or agencies.

Nowadays it is important to write a focused CV bringing to the fore the evidence the recruiter is looking for with regard to skills, qualifications and experience, making sure this evidence is quick to find on your CV and stands out so the recruiter can find it in less than 15 seconds. Once you have gained their attention, they may spend several minutes reading your CV, but the trick is to get their attention quickly so they will read on.

Our advice is to:

>Treat the job advertisement as an exam question
>Treat your CV as the answer paper

By doing so, you are writing a focused CV that should mean your suitability for a role is not missed.

If you follow this thought process through you will realise that:

The interview is the spoken or oral exam… (covered in our Interview Guide)

So if a job advertisement states that you must have 'excellent customer service skills', your CV needs to highlight this skill to the recruiter (if you do have them). But it is not enough to simply state 'excellent customer service skills'. The obvious next question is 'why do you say that?' By not including the evidence to substantiate the statement, the impact of highlighting the skill is lost, so try to support your initial statement with evidence, such as: 'Excellent customer service skills having worked in customer-facing roles for over 10 years'.

Later we will show you how to incorporate these statements into your CV to make the most impact.

Recent students / returners to work

For those new to the job market or returning to the job market after a break, you may be unable to provide work-based evidence to back up your claim to a skill. In this case it might be necessary to highlight the skill required such as 'teamwork', and instead of drawing upon work experience, highlight your ability by providing other evidence, such as being a keen sportsperson or having actively participated in team activities at school / college.

Themed CVs / multiple CVs

Many people often have experience in several areas and can apply for differing job roles. Often they will try and write one CV to use when applying for these differing roles and expect recruiters to find what they are looking for in the CV. But, as stated earlier, you need to focus your CV towards one type of role.

Ideally then, rather than having one CV where everything is jumbled up, we suggest writing several focused themed CVs. This does not mean dropping other skill areas from your CV, merely bringing to the fore the most relevant evidence for a particular role.

Graduates / ex-students

Many ex-students are unsure of what they would like to do next. If this is the case, you may need several CVs, one written for each area of employment interest. It is worth spending the time writing these CVs, as by doing so you are demonstrating to a potential employer an interest in an area of employment.

We suggest, however, that you try to focus upon a few job roles and employment sectors, as it may help produce better results.

Tailor your CV

Once you have your CV / CVs written – which may take several hours – it is then important to remember that these are merely templates and need to be further worked on for each application. It is important that your CV is tailored to specific applications and reflects the experience required by the job advertisement.

Even if a job advertisement is similar to a previous one you have seen, it may have subtle variations and the CV needs to reflect them. Going back to our analogy:

Job advertisement = the exam question; CV = the answer paper

If the exam question is slightly different, should your answer not be different also?

In the past people did not need to tailor their CV so much, instead sending in a tailored covering letter. Unfortunately, this does not work as well since the invention of email and online applications. Covering letters are often ignored in the first sift, with recruiters going straight for your CV as it should highlight the skills they are looking for.

Also, being practical: 50 applications = 50 CVs; 50 covering letters. How do recruiters cut down their workload by half? Ignore the covering letters.

However, this does not mean you should not send a covering letter. Once past the first screening and at line manager stage, the line managers are interested in what your covering letter says.

Key skill statements / CV profiles

CV profiles started to appear in the 1990s and are on almost everyone's CVs these days. They are paragraphs usually at the top of a CV that try to tell the reader how good you are. Sample profiles can be found on many websites and most get you to highlight soft skills such as:

'A hard-working reliable individual who is quick to learn; has excellent customer service and communication skills; is able to work both independently and as part of a team'

The problem is that most are full of soft skills, very similar in content, and volume recruiters will often not even bother reading them as a result. Would you if they all say the same thing?

In short, then, these generic fluffy profiles do not work and by including them you are wasting part of your 'shop window' – the top half of your CV where you can gain most impact.

Instead of using a profile we suggest using the baked beans trick…

In the supermarket, you know you have a tin of beans in your hand because in large letters it says 'baked beans'. If you want to know what is in the tin and why it claims to be a tin full of baked beans, you turn it over and read the ingredients.

Use the same trick on your own CV; a headline to identify the role the CV is aimed at and short bullet points underneath to highlight your relevant skills, experience etc.

For example:

Experienced Warehouse Operative / Fork Lift Truck Driver

- **10 years' experience including Goods-In, Order Picking & Packing**
- **FLT Reach & Counterbalance Licences – loading and unloading lorries along with placing stock into the high racking**

The banner headline clearly highlights the role the CV is aimed at. The bullet points then expand on the headline providing supporting facts and answer the questions an interviewer would ask you if you turned up for an interview without your CV.

The headline says an experienced warehouse operative, so if applying for a warehouse role, what questions would the interviewer ask:

- Have you worked in a warehouse before? – Yes, for 10 years
- Doing what? – Goods-in, order picking and order packing
- We also need a FLT operator, what licences do you have? – Reach and counterbalance

Once you have highlighted the relevant experience, it is important to highlight some of the softer skills required by the role, such as good team player; excellent customer service skills; able to organise and prioritise your workload.

Because these are 'framed' by the hard skills and practical experience and the statement highlighting 10 years' experience, although you might not provide evidence to back up these claims, it is assumed they were developed over the 10 years working in the warehouse. This means you can add in:

Experienced Warehouse Operative / Fork Lift Truck Driver

- **10 years' experience including Goods-In, Order Picking & Packing**
- **FLT Reach & Counterbalance Licences – loading and unloading lorries along with placing stock into the high racking**
- **Track record of consistently hitting set targets and deadlines**
- **Excellent customer service skills; strong team player**
- **Able to effectively organise and prioritise workload**

Note we use the term *excellent* customer service skills rather than average, OK or reasonable... a CV is there to sell you to get an interview. In retail they always highlight in their adverts excellent customer service skills, so do not be afraid to use the same language when describing your own ability.

If you get the bullet points right, will the recruiter actually need to read the rest of your CV?

Remember, bullet points are short and punchy statements and should not – unless absolutely necessary – be more than 2 lines long.

Include generic job titles / job title variations / buzz words

We will look at CV databases later in this guide, but another point to note is that recruiters searching a CV database for candidates will tend to search under generic job titles. This means that, if your actual job title is vague, remember to include on your CV the generic variation. One way to do this is to include the generic version after your actual title in brackets:

Telephone response handling manager (contact centre manager)

It is also important to include job title variations on your CV. An accounts clerk could also be known as a finance assistant. By including both job titles on your CV you will appear in both searches by a recruiter on a CV database.

When adding in titles remember to include actual job titles rather than refer to a skill area. A recruiter would not search using the term 'administration' when looking for an administrator as many people could have this word on their CV. Only someone who is an administrator is likely to have the job title on their CV.

Another issue people often have is that their job title does not accurately represent what they actually did. You may easily be rejected for a role because the recruiter interprets what your role was incorrectly. The way to get around this is to highlight the actual role job title in brackets after your real job title:

Account Director (Internal Sales)
Accounts Assistant (Business Analyst) – real example from the BBC

Finally, in addition to job titles, include the buzz words. These are words recruiters may use to further refine their searches on CV databases. Buzz words could be IT packages; industry jargon; equipment types; or words specific to a role.

As CV database search engines are getting more sophisticated, many have started to rank a CV based upon these buzz words and expected phrases and jargon included on a CV. This can in some cases have a great impact on where your CV appears in recruiters' CV search results: a CV with the jargon appearing in search

© Job Doctor

results on page 1; without the jargon on page 37 = 370th position with 10 results per page.

Use brackets to highlight specific experience

As part of a role, you may have had experience in an area which you would now like to concentrate on or highlight. Your job title may not imply this experience was part of your role. Again, by using brackets, you can alter the perception of the recruiter about your role:

IT Director (Project Manager)

Thus highlighting project management was a key part of your job role.

Use the word 'seeking'

If you are looking for a role and have little experience in that area, such as a graduate looking for their first job or if looking to change careers, you cannot include on your CV a statement such as:

Accounts Clerk with 5 years' experience

So instead use the term 'seeking' in your headline:

Seeking a role as an Accounts Clerk / Finance Assistant

By doing so you will appear in search results and also highlight to the recruiter that you have thought about the role you would like to do. Next, you need to highlight each skill area required and try to support this with some evidence. For instance:

Seeking a role as an Accounts Clerk / Finance Assistant

- **Excellent numerical skills with high attention to detail: achieved A* Grades in Maths and Science subjects**
- **Strong team players: on School Hockey and Netball Teams**
- **Highly committed – passed all course modules first time**
- **Quick to learn and with a passion to follow a career in finance**

You will notice that the last line highlights a passion for finance. Although unsupported with evidence, this says to a recruiter this individual knows what they want to do. In reality a job seeker unsure of their career path may have 10 of these CVs stating a passion for numerous employment areas, but it is only this CV the recruiter will hopefully see.

Structuring the rest of your CV

As previously stated, the top half of the CV is your shop window, so use it to highlight relevant experience. Other expected sections that should be on your CV include:

- Work History / Employment History
- Education
- Training – shows ongoing personal development
- Other information – which can include hobbies and interests; IT Skills; Full Clean Driving Licence etc.

Work history / employment history

When detailing your work history, start by highlighting the company's name, your job titles and the dates of employment so they stand out clearly on your CV – possibly use bold; raised font; or underlining. This is important throughout your CV to make it easy to move between sections quickly and more logical to follow. It also makes your CV easier for a volume recruiter to 'scan read'.

Under each company start by including a short introduction to what the business does. It is not always necessary to include this introduction as people know who Google are, but which part of Google did you work in?

Next, include a short introduction or overview of what your role entailed. Imagine you are at a party and someone asks you what you do for a living. Hopefully you would not bore the person, but provide a short and to-the-point overview; ideally 3 or 4 lines long to position your skills and experience.

An error people often make is to launch straight into a long list of duties under their job title that need to be read and mentally added together to understand what they did in a role. By including a short introduction or overview of your role, it becomes easy and quick for the recruiter to understand what your role involved. It is also easy to alter this short overview when tailoring your CV to different roles.

Now, underneath the introduction to the business and your role, include achievements rather than duties next. The recruiter has a fair idea from the introduction about what you were doing, so now grab them by telling them how good you were in the role and what you achieved...

Achievements

Achievement can be as simple as: 'consistently hit set targets and deadlines' or 'worked to high levels of accuracy'.

Achievements often start with an action word and may include the benefit to the business. If including the business benefit, to make the most impact it is often best to highlight the benefit to the business first – the 'how' second.

© Job Doctor

So instead of: 'Introduced a number of new working practices that resulted in a 250K saving', highlight the positive outcome first: 'Saved the company £250K by introducing new working practices'.

Achievements also do not need to be huge:

- Appointed as the main point of contact for key clients turning over £50K+
- Consistently delivered excellent customer service even when working under pressure and to tight deadlines
- Effectively planned my workload to ensure daily targets were met
- Became product champion for the new xxxxx range
- Consistently achieved set targets & SLAs
- Increased sales within 'client A' by 50% over a 3-year period
- Won and developed several new clients, growing the business by over 50%
- Achieved high quality scores in internal audits in relation to customer records
- Ensured all contractual administration and data protection procedures are adhered to as set by SLAs (Service Level Agreements)
- Achieved 100% accuracy when updating files and records
- Effectively coordinated the introduction of a new timesheet logging system
- Increased the customer satisfaction score by over 10% through the introduction of in-house training (management)
- Increased productivity within my team through staff training and introducing a buddying system
- Significantly increased my team's performance through the introduction of new working practices

If you can quantify the results, this helps, but to merely state an overall positive benefit is often enough to impress the reader. To help write achievement statements we have included a list of suggested action words at the end of the CV writing section.

Duties and responsibilities

After your achievements, you need to include your duties and responsibilities. Try to highlight first those that are most relevant for the role applied for. Also try to include the detail, and remember – you may understand what your role entailed, but the recruiter may not and you need to state actual facts and duties.

For example: in accounts roles the individual will often carry reconciliations. If this is not stated on the CV, the recruiter may not realise this was part of your role, however do not go to the other extreme and start including miniscule details.

Education

It is not necessary to list all your qualifications if they are 'old' – in fact many people leave qualifications gained at school off their CV. As the years go by, the qualifications awarded have changed and they can often identify to a recruiter your potential age.

Also, who cares about qualifications over 20 years old, even over 10 years old if not vocational? As stated earlier, education is now often relegated to the bottom of your CV rather than being at the top, but still reference in the top bullet points relevant qualifications that will help support your application.

Recent students, however, should keep education near the top of the CV, unless they have some solid relevant work history.

Shorten your CV / de-ageing your CV

A simple trick to help keep a CV short is to only include full details on job roles you held in the last 10 to 15 years. One way to do this is to summarise older job roles, keeping in the summary and specific experience you feel is relevant as required:

> **Prior to 2000**
> Employed as: Accounts Clerk, Finance Assistant and Junior Accountant

If you have some experience within a previous role, or even if you feel it is important to highlight you worked for a particular business, include this detail in the summary.

De-ageing a CV

Another benefit of not including the detail with regards older jobs along with the employment dates is that you are also de-aging your CV.

When de-aging your CV, make sure other details are also removed. For instance, dates relating to school / college / university should also be removed. Also as qualifications awarded have changed, it might be useful to also remove reference to the older qualifications. In the UK, polytechnics were renamed universities, so potentially change the establishment details to the new university name also.

Sample CVs and CV headlines

To help pull all our advice together, we have provided on the next few pages a few examples of CVs and CV headlines. The examples are there to demonstrate how content should be laid out, and the CV samples we are providing are not necessarily the most visually appealing CVs with regard to layout. We therefore suggest you find a CV layout that you like on the Internet, then use our templates as a guide to maximise the impact of the contents. When you have finished altering your CV, print off a hard copy and assess whether the overall layout is appealing; visual appearance is also important as discussed earlier.

You will also see that we may include achievements in the bullet points under the CV headline , as they can help add value and highlight a specific skill. Depending on the role, their inclusion can help to impress the reader.

Garry James

Address: 55 Arian Court
St Thomas' Drive
Any Town
Middlesex HA5 4SR

Email: garry@htr-hr.co.uk

Mobile Tel: xxxxxx xxxxxxxxx

Home Tel: 0201 xxxxxxxx

Experienced Warehouse Operative / Fork Lift Truck Driver

- **10 years' experience including Goods-In, Order Picking & Packing**
- **FLT Reach & Counter Balance Licences – loading and unloading lorries along with placing stock into the high racking**
- **Qualified First Aid Certificate and Fire Marshall**
- **Food Hygiene NVQ Level 1**
- **Excellent team player, self-motivated and quick to learn**

(LIST JOB TITLES & JOB TITLE VARIATIONS IN THE HEADLINE TO BE FOUND IN RECRUITERS' SEARCHES ON CV DATABASES; INCLUDE A FEW POINTS UNDERNEATH TO SUMMARISE YOUR EXPERIENCE – TAILOR THIS TO INDIVIDUAL JOBS. TOP HALF OF A CV = YOUR SHOP WINDOW.)

EMPLOYMENT HISTORY

2005 – Present   Roy's Transport and Distribution Ltd
Warehouse Operative (FLT Operator)

Roy's Transport work for Nisa Food Stores distributing food and non-food products to their retail stores; my role was based in the main warehouse where orders were picked prior to store delivery.
(PROVIDE AN OVERVIEW OF THE BUSINESS – IDENTIFIES TO THE READER INDUSTRY SECTOR / SIZE OF BUSINESS)

For the last 6 years I have worked in the goods-in area unloading lorries using a FLT, and also covered in the picking and packing areas during busy periods.
(BRIEF OVERVIEW OF YOUR ROLE AS AN INTRODUCTION)

Achievements:
➢ Consistently achieved daily targets and picking deadlines
➢ 100% safety record when operating the Reach Truck in tight racking
➢ Working to high levels of accuracy while picking store orders
➢ (INCLUDE 5 OR 6 AT MOST)

Responsibilities:
➢ Unloading lorries as they arrive using a Counter Balance FLT

- Moving the stock into the warehouse and placing it onto the high racking using a Reach FLT
- Scanning the barcodes and logging the stock into the warehouse computerised stock management system
- Carrying out general clean up duties within the warehouse
- Helping to pick individual Nisa Store orders and shrink wrapping pallets once complete
- Printed off the delivery paperwork to send to dispatch.

1998 – 2005   **Self Employed Gardener / Landscaper**

General garden maintenance including cutting lawns, clearing rubbish, trimming hedges *(IF THE JOB ROLE IS NOT RELEVANT TO THE TYPE OF WORK BEING SOUGHT, INCLUDE SOME DETAILS BUT NO NEED TO GO INTO GREAT DEPTH. POSSIBLY INCLUDE ACHIEVEMENTS FOR THE ROLE AS AN ALTERNATIVE TO HIGHLIGHT A SKILL YOU DEVELOPED THERE)*

Prior to 1998

Various general labouring and factory jobs

(JOBS OVER 15 TO 20 YEARS AGO ARE PROBABLY NOT RELEVANT TO A NEW EMPLOYER, SO ONE TRICK IS TO MERELY SUMMARISE AN OVERVIEW OF THE JOB ROLES. THIS CAN ALSO HELP TO DE-AGE A CV)

EDUCATION AND TRAINING

1990   **3 A Levels:** Biology, Physics & General Studies
1988   **10 GSCEs:** Including Mathematics and English Language

(IF TRYING TO DE-AGE A CV, REMOVE THE EDUCATION DATES ABOVE)

Courses attended in recent years include:

> Health & Safety in the Warehouse
> FLT Certification on Reach and Counterbalance FLT Trucks
> Pallet Truck basic safety
> First Aid (Certified First Aider)
> Fire Marshall Training – 2 years as a Fire Marshall at Roy's Transport
> Safe Lifting Practices
> Food Hygiene NVQ Level 1

ADDITIONAL INFORMATION

Good IT Skills including: Microsoft Word, Excel, and PowerPoint. Also experience of in-house stock management systems whilst at Roy's Transport

I enjoy watching and playing sports, especially football and golf.

Sample CV headlines – for individuals with relevant experience

Teaching assistant

> **Currently seeking a role as Teaching Assistant / Classroom Assistant / Learning Support Assistant (LSA) – Teaching Assistant NVQ Level 3**

- 9 months' current teaching experience with 4 to 11-year-olds
- 4 years' previous experience in schools
- Supported KS1 and KS2 in Literacy and Numeracy
- 1-2-1 and Group Support; including after-school activities
- Special needs support working with: dyslexia; dyspraxia; autism; SEN; ADHD; disability
- Supporting the teacher with arts lessons (highly artistic)
- Excellent communication and pupil engagement skills

Accounts assistant

> **Experienced Finance Assistant / Accounts Clerk with 15 years' experience (AAT Level 3 Qualification)**

- Worked in fast-moving organisations - SMEs and large companies turning over £250K to £10m
- Sage Line 50 experience includes: Sales Ledger; Purchase Ledger; Credit Control; Payroll; Stock
- Weekly & Monthly Payroll (up to 65 staff) - SSP; Deductions; PAYE; Overtime & Expenses
- Proficient in: SAP; Syspro; Vebra; Sage Line 100; Sage Line 200; Sage Line 500, Excel; Word; PowerPoint
- Good team player, self-motivated and quick to learn

Engineering

> **Process Engineer with 11 years' experience within industrial scale manufacturing**

- Comprehensive experience in engineering with skills in process improvement, data analysis and solutions advice
- Master of Engineering with Honours in Chemical Engineering
- Strong expertise in problem-solving and ensuring tests and trials are easily understood, products are performing properly, and products are reliable
- International experience having worked across EMEA
- Excellent customer service skills having worked on client sites including: xxxx
- Consistently exceeds organisational goals and expectations

Project manager

IT Project Manager with over 16 years' experience

- Delivered a range of projects across multi-functional areas including: Supply Chain, Production, Finance, Customer Services, Sales, Marketing, EHS, Technical Services, Human Resources
- Industry experience includes: Financial Services, Manufacturing, Utilities
- Track record of delivering complex projects on time and within budget
- Experience with ERP, CRM and portal systems
- PMP Accredited (PMI / PMBOK); Waterfall; Agile; ITIL; working knowledge of Prince2; very proficient in planning with Microsoft Project
- Headed up project teams of up to 50 staff
- UK and European-based project delivery across over 10 sites and 500 staff
- Controlled project scope, budget, risk, quality and procurement
- Strong Vendor and Stakeholder Management skills

Accountant

Chartered Management Accountant with 20+ years' experience

- Extensive experience of business and financial strategy; financial modelling; and working closely with operational areas
- Key player in the senior management team
- Fully accountable for the day-to-day operations of businesses turning over between £1m and £50m
- Successfully implemented and project-managed a number of key changes to business operations resulting in increased efficiencies
- Performance-managed teams of up to 8 staff across 3 sites

Administrator / receptionist

Receptionist / Administrator with over 10 years' experience

- Excellent customer service skills, good at building rapport with people
- Well-presented, polite, and a good communicator
- Confident and flexible member of any team, maintaining a high standard at all times; high attention to detail
- Well-organised individual who works well under own initiative
- Works well in demanding and difficult situations – previously employed as a medical practice receptionist
- Bilingual: English and Punjabi
- IT skills: familiar with MS Office and other IT packages (ECDL)

Facilities manager

Facilities Supervisor / Facilities Assistant with over 20 years' experience

- Provided effective support to line managers on facility issues: repairs, office moves, health & safety, postal services, car fleet maintenance
- Awarded the 'Unsung Heroes' award (2012)
- Identified cost savings of over £100K in copy and print costs
- Effectively negotiated with suppliers to bring down cost whist increasing quality
- Co-ordinated and managed all third-party activity and contractors
- Worked to tight and exacting deadlines, ensuring all repairs were carried out within the set timeframes
- An enthusiastic, self-motivated, responsible, reliable and hardworking individual

Sales

Sales Executive / Business Development Manager over 7 years' experience

- Proven track record of achieving / exceeding targets & deadlines – Top Sales Person Award 2014
- 80% new business; 20% account management
- Sector experience include: utilities; telecoms; training services
- Instrumental in launching a new product into the telecoms market in 2013, resulting in sales in excess of €600K per year
- Highly organised and able to prioritise own workload
- Strong relationship management skills; good at winning and keeping business

Production / manufacturing

Production Operative / Factory Worker with 20 years' experience

- Worked on lines producing PCB boards; cable looms; and where hand tools were required in the assembly (hand-soldering etc.)
- High attention to detail with a focus on producing high quality intricate items
- Able to effectively prioritise and organise my workload; used to working under pressure and to targets / deadlines
- Leadership skills having deputised for the supervisor during weekend shifts
- Punctual, reliable, and able to work on my own initiative as well as working well within a team

Mechanical / electrical engineer

| HV Construction/Site Manager with 15 years' experience in the installation of Electrical/Mechanical Switchgear |

- **C&G Electrical Engineering 236 Parts 1 & 2;**
- **Vast experience in LV-MV-HV systems**
- **Scottish Power authorised to WI-1, EN-1& WL-1**
- **Worked on: Railways, Power Stations, Offshore Installations**
- **Responsible for: Planning, Procurement, Tendering and Installation**
- **Excellent working knowledge of Risk Assessments, Method Statements and Audit Assessments**
- **Track record of effectively managing employees and sub-contractors in both Electrical and Civil disciplines**
- **Ensures all KPIs and deadlines are met**
- **Good background in H&S, Quality Assurance, Systems Documentation**

Retail manager

| Retail Manager with over 20 years' experience within a fast-moving retail operation |

- **Performance-managed teams of up to 15 staff**
- **Track record of developing a culture of excellent customer service within my teams**
- **In-depth knowledge of store operations including: recruitment; training; stock management; cash handling; key holder; work schedules**
- **Increased sales from €20K/week to over €35K/week over a 6-month period**
- **An inspirational leader who leads by example and achieves results**
- **NVQ in Retail Management Level 3**

IT software engineer

| Software Engineer / Software Developer with over 10 years' experience |

- **Python 3 with object-oriented programming (expert); Bourne and Bash shell scripting (expert); Java and C# (expert)**
- **Worked within technical teams developing bespoke financial software systems**
- **Extensive experience with software life cycle and continuous process improvement, including Agile process and Quality Assurance (ISO 9001)**
- **Worked closely with the sales team and key client contacts to identify and scope software projects and client needs, and to establish SLAs**

(Note – With IT CVs, underneath the headline and bullet points we often see listed all the technology the individual has experience of, including operating systems, IT packages used etc. These are listed under the heading 'IT Skills' before the employment details)

Personal assistant / office manager

Over 15 years PA experience supporting Senior Managers / Directors

- Strong office management / personal assistant / human resources background (CIPD Associate)
- Diary management; hotel bookings; stationary ordering; supervising junior staff; facilities management
- Track record of consistently delivering excellent customer service; NVQ Level 3 in Customer Service
- Excellent communication skills both verbal and written
- Good telephone manner, professional, dedicated, flexible attitude
- Strong attention to detail, problem-solving and meeting deadlines

Human resources

HR Generalist / Senior HR Officer / Human Resources Manager with over 10 years' experience

- Extensive knowledge of employment law including: grievance; disciplinary
- Recruitment; Training; Assessment Centre design and delivery
- Talent management and succession planning
- Employee Relations (including Union negotiations)
- Strong manufacturing and commercial background
- Post Graduate Diploma in Human Resource Management; BA (Hons) Human Resource Management & Business IT
- Able to work closely with key managers, often in demanding situations

Customer service

Customer Service Advisor with over 5 years' experience

- Track record of delivering excellent customer service at all times
- High attention to detail, able to prioritise effectively
- Excellent communication skills – face-to-face; telephone and email / letter
- Proficient in Microsoft Office Word; Excel; PowerPoint; Access; Outlook and bespoke software packages
- Multilingual: fluent in English, Bengali, Hindi and Urdu
- Smart appearance
- Calm when under pressure

Student / graduate / school leaver CVs

The CV examples above are for those with experience. If you do not have this experience in an area, you need to 'paint a picture' of what you can offer the employer instead.

A key part of this is to make sure your CV clearly highlights to the employer that you have a keen interest in a job type, are focused upon the role you are applying for, and where possible provide evidence of ability even if this is from non-work based evidence.

Start by using a headline such as: **Currently seeking a role as a xxx**

This clearly highlights that your application is focused and that you have a conviction to achieve a role as an xxx.

Underneath, use the same bullet point layout as before to highlight the skills required by the role, and as best as you can, provide evidence as to whether it is from school / college / university or from social activities or even short placements.

In addition, you can strengthen your application by including a short personal statement in your CV. Unlike a personal profile, a personal statement is used to convey an interest in an area of employment or to explain something away if changing career (looked at next). It is a short sales pitch, and will identify to a recruiter why you are interested in a role.

The personal profile is placed under the CV heading and bullet points before the education. As an example:

Apprentice application

Seeking an Apprenticeship in Engineering

- Quick to learn, hard-working and adaptable in approach
- Good academic ability: 6 GCSEs grade A-C, including Maths, English and Science
- Currently studying BTEC ICT and BTEC Business Studies (predicted Distinction grade in both)
- Good communication skills having experienced the retail environment working with both younger and older people; also assisted with school open days
- Strong team player: Awarded Junior & Senior School Colours for team events
- Active helper in the Sikh community at the local Temple on many Sundays (Sevah)

Personal Statement

I have always enjoyed practical activities including DIY and helping out my friends with jobs that need doing. Having thought about a potential career path, I have decided that I would like to follow a career in engineering. I believe I have a mature attitude with the desire to succeed and develop my skills, making me an asset to an employer.

To show how this builds into a full CV:

Sample school leaver CV

Richard James

34 Warburton Road, Epsom, Surrey SU35 9ST
Tel: 07973 XXX XXX   Email: richard@htr-hr.co.uk   Age 18 years
Full Clean Driving Licence – Own transport

Seeking a job in retail as Retail Assistant / Shop Assistant

- **Quick to learn, hard-working and adaptable in approach: good academic achievement with Grades A to B in my A Levels; 9 GCSEs inc. Maths & English**
- **Good communication skills having been on the debating team at school and helping to run weekly meetings and events**
- **High level of commitment and goal-oriented having successfully completed my Duke of Edinburgh Silver Award**
- **Able to deal with people of all ages; worked in Marks and Spencer as part of my school work placement**
- **Strong team player having been awarded School Colours for school team events; keen footballer**

Personal Statement

Having recently completed my A Levels I now wish to start a career in retail. I enjoy working with people which I feel is important in this role along with working as part of a team. My school placement was with Marks and Spencer for a week; this provided me with a good insight into how a shop works; also providing practical skills such as shelf stocking and labelling goods. It also gave me the opportunity to deal with members of the public and an appreciation of how good customer service is so important in retail.

IN THE SPACES ABOVE, YOU NEED TO HIGHLIGHT WHAT JOB ROLE YOU WISH TO FOLLOW, THEN HIGHLIGHT WHAT SKILLS AND EXPERIENCE YOU FEEL YOU HAVE FOR THE ROLE. THE ABOVE HAS USED BULLET POINTS TO HIGHLIGHT COMMUNICATION / ACADEMIC ABILITY / COMMITMENT (TARGET-DRIVEN) AND TEAM WORKING. THE PERSONAL STATEMENT IS USED TO RE-INFORCE YOUR JOB CHOICE BY HIGHLIGHTING A 'DESIRE' TO FOLLOW A CAREER IN RETAIL AND THE INSIGHT GAINED AS PART OF A SCHOOL PLACEMENT.

Education

North Surrey College   **2009 – 2016**

A Levels – Biology A; Geography B; Business Studies A
GCSEs – Maths B; English Language B; English Literature B; Science B; Additional Science B; Business Studies C; Design Technology C; History C; Geography C

Work History

ANY WORK HISTORY NEEDS TO BE LISTED, HOWEVER SMALL.

Other Information / Interests

I have completed my Silver Duke of Edinburgh Award and this involved learning new life skills such as cooking and driving a car; numerous physical challenges, camping expeditions, long distance walks in the Lake District and community/voluntary activities.

I have been awarded both Junior and Senior School Colours for team sports including being on the school's 1st team in football. In the lower school I was Deputy School Captain, and in the 6th form House Captain for the School along with being a Prefect.

I enjoy golf, hill walking, and computer gaming in my spare time along with playing football. I was an active member of a local football team for over 6 years, playing in the local football league.

INTERESTS AND OTHER INFORMATION NEEDS TO NOT FOCUS UPON 'SOCIALISING', BUT TRY TO HIGHLIGHT ANY ACHIEVEMENTS OR ACTIVITIES THAT SHOW YOU AS A 'ROUNDED' PERSON = NOT ONLY ACADEMIC BUT THAT YOU OFFER A MORE PRACTICAL SET OF SKILLS ALSO.

What if you have little experience to include as evidence?

As you can see by the layout above, the 'shop window' of the CV is heavily focused on highlighting skills and experience whilst the personal statement is a mini sales pitch. You may not have experience of participating in sports etc., in which case use the personal statement to highlight a keenness / passion for a role:

Personal statement – entry level warehouse role

Having had a week's work experience in a warehouse carrying out general duties, along with always enjoying physical activities such football and the gym, I have decided I would like to follow a career in a warehouse. I offer enthusiasm along with the commitment to do a good job. I am flexible with regard to hours worked and duties I perform, and will always give 100% to anything I do.

Personal statement – entry level horticulture role

Working as a gardener and having a love for plants, I am keen to follow a career in horticulture. I love working outdoors and get great satisfaction from growing plants. I am quick to learn and will always commit to completing any task that I am responsible for to a very high standard. I am punctual, reliable and well-mannered and would describe myself as outgoing, sociable and a good team player

<u>Graduate CV</u>

Graduate CVs use a similar layout to the CV above for an entry level position. The main difference is that you would include under the bullet points and personal statement your education and details about your degree.

If the degree content is relevant to the role applied for it is important to list subjects and options studied as the degree can be viewed as 3 years of subject training. Try not to list just subject headings such as 'Management Accounts' (finance roles). Instead expand on this to highlight areas covered such as – bank and petty cash reconciliation's, trial balance, sales and purchase ledger.

You can also include under the top headline reference to your knowledge gained:

Seeking a role as an Accounts Clerk / Finance Assistant having just graduated with a BA (Hons) 2:2 in Business and Finance

- Good understanding of accounts gained during my course including: profit and loss accounts; balance sheets; sales and purchase ledgers
- Strong IT skills: Sage Line 50; Microsoft Excel (advanced); Word; PowerPoint

Underneath the headlines and bullet points next include a 'Personal Statement' highlighting your desire to follow your chosen career path as it strengthens your application – even include words like 'desire' and 'passion'.

<u>Graduates not looking to follow a career related to their degree / general degrees</u>

If the degree is being used as a general degree, you may be better off highlighting what you learned as part of your degree under the degree heading, or aspects of your degree that show personal development. For instance, highlighting a good mark for a 15,000-word dissertation would show literacy skills and imply ability.

In addition use your personal statement to highlight the fact you studied the subject out of interest and what you feel you gained from your studies. For instance:

<u>Personal statement – graduate seeking a career in retail</u>

Having always been a people person I studied Psychology at university with the intention of using this as a general degree. Since graduating I have had the opportunity to work as a volunteer in retail; I loved the interaction with customers and thrived in this role. I have therefore decided to follow a full-time career in retail with the aim of progressing into management. I feel I can offer an employer a high level of commitment and a professional attitude.

The following highlights the structure of a graduate CV where they are not looking to follow a career in the subject they studied at university:

Helen Jones B.A. Hons (2:1)

Address: 55 Arian Court
St Thomas' Drive
Any Town
Middlesex HA5 4SR

Age: 23 years

Email: helenj@htr-hr.co.uk

Mobile Tel: xxxxxx xxxxxxxxx

Home Tel: 0201 xxxxxxxx

Seeking a role as a Support Worker / Care Worker having completed my degree in Psychology

- Excellent people and customer service skills, having worked part time in a bar for just under 3 years whilst studying
- Previously supported a family member during a period of illness: washing and bathing; cooking and feeding; general household duties
- A caring and empathetic nature with a desire to exceed expectations
- Hard-working; adaptable and quick to learn
- Strong team player having played on hockey teams for over 6 years
- Excellent IT and written skills

Personal Statement

Having always been a people person, I studied Psychology at university with the intention of using this as a general degree. Since graduating I have had the opportunity to work as a volunteer in an old-age home; I loved the interaction with residents and thrived in this role. I have therefore decided to follow a full-time career in care with the aim of progressing into management. I feel I can offer an employer a high level of commitment, along with a flexible and professional attitude.

EDUCATION

Lancaster University 2013 – 2016   B.A. Hons (2:1) Psychology

Completed as part of my degree a 10,000-word dissertation requiring extensive study; awarded a high 2:1. In addition I undertook several group assignments, acting as team leader on many.

John Westwood School
You may wish to put other qualifications including subjects and grades here, or they can be placed under 'Other Information' at the end of the CV.

EMPLOYMENT HISTORY

Terry Wine Bar   **Part Time Waiter**   **2011 – 2013**

Worked in a busy bar whilst a student. Consistently delivered excellent customer service and often took charge of the bar whilst the owner was at the cash and carry. In addition, I would help cash up at the end of the night and train up more junior members of staff.

OTHER INFORMATION

Excellent IT Skills: Microsoft Word; Excel; PowerPoint; Access; Photoshop; Publisher.

I have completed my Outward Bound Silver Award and this involved learning new life skills such as cooking and driving a car; undertaking numerous physical challenges such as camping expeditions, long distance walks in the mountains and community / voluntary activities.

I enjoy golf, hill walking, and computer gaming in my spare time along with playing hockey. I was an active member of a local hockey team for over 6 years, playing in the local hockey league.

On our graduate template above you will note that employment history has slipped to page 2, but to ensure the reader knows about the bar experience this is highlighted on Page 1 as part of the bullet points at the top.

When you get to employment history and the bar role, the description is not about stacking glasses or taking payments; but about the skills an employer might want.

> 'Worked in a busy bar whilst a student. Consistently delivered excellent customer service and often took charge of the bar whilst the owner was at the cash and carry. In addition, I would help cash up at the end of the night and train up more junior members of staff.'

The description highlights several achievements:

- Ability to work under pressure
- Ability to deliver excellent customer service
- Ability to work as part of a team
- Ability to take a role of responsibility by looking after the bar while the boss was away and training up new staff members
- Being trusted – by her boss allowing her to deputise
- Ability to work as part of a team and support team members
- Also, although not an achievement, good numerical skills

On the CV three short lines, but when used well, highlight impressive skills!

Career changers / sideways move CVs

If you are looking to change career direction, the reasons why you are applying for the role in question are often highlighted in your covering letter. However, with recruiters often not reading your covering letter but going straight to the CV, these reasons can be missed, with the recruiter likely to reject your application as a result.

To get around this, a personal statement can again be used to highlight on your CV why you are looking to change direction or specialise in a specific area:

Complete change of direction from retail to administration

Over the last few years whilst working in retail, I have enjoyed the interaction with people and also been heavily involved in the paperwork / administration side of running the shop. I have really enjoyed this aspect of my role and have decided that I would like to move into a more office-based role, also having excellent IT skills. I feel I can offer an employer excellent written and verbal communication skills along with vast experience in customer service. I am a strong team player, very organised, and able to prioritise work effectively.

Moving into a project management role after heading an IT department

A major part of my role as Head of IT for the last 10 years' has been focused upon delivering projects into the business, and I now wish to specialise and move into a project management role full-time. My role has seen me run project teams of up to 30 across multiple sites, with budgets of between €20K and €200K. I have been responsible for projects full lifecycle including: planning; risk; troubleshooting; and stakeholder management.

Now looking to move to a lower level position

Having been recently made redundant, I have decided that I no longer wish to work as a customer service team leader, and I would like to return to the role of Customer Service Advisor. I have always loved the interaction with people, and this is something I have missed as a team leader. I have excellent people and organisational skills; always aiming to deliver the highest level of customer service. In addition, I have a strong work ethic and an excellent timekeeping record.

By including a personal statement on your CV you can use it to highlight to a recruiter your desire to have a complete career change. You may not, however, be effectively highlighting your transferable skills – skills gained in one area that are applicable and useful for other roles.

Another CV type which can help an individual change career or help them repackage themselves is a function or skill-based CV. These focus upon and bring to the fore transferable skills.

© Job Doctor

Functional CVs

As an alternative to a standard biographical CV, another style of CV is a Skill-Based or Functional CV. These CVs focus upon transferable skills and can be far more powerful in convincing an interviewer that you are right for a job role.

The focus is upon skillset first, your job titles second. Rather than be pre-judged based on your job title, and potentially rejected because your job title does not imply you have the right background, they reposition you as a set of relevant skills.

Functional CVs are useful if you are:

1)   A Contractor / Interim Manager, allowing you to summarise areas of ability
2)   Looking to make a total career change, thus repackaging yourself
3)   Wanting to highlight specific skills and experience
4)   Looking to 'slip time' and highlight older experience first
5)   A recent graduate looking to bring evidence together from courses / jobs

A functional CV will summarise your experience under skill headings such as 'Project Management' or 'Customer Service' or 'Teamwork'. This evidence may be not just from one job role, but often from several, even going back several years, with your career history appearing often on page 2 of the CV.

They switch the focus towards your transferable skills.

The problem with functional CVs is that they have to be bespoke: written to the precise job requirements. This is where most people go wrong. Because it takes so much time to keep altering the CV, job hunters produce one CV with a list of skill headings and send it to a recruiter hoping the recruiter will spot the ones they are looking for. They have not got the time. So it is vital to really analyse the job role, identify the relevant skills for the role, and provide precise evidence under those skill headings.

As stated above – if used well functional CVs are very powerful at highlighting to a recruiter that you are right for a role, providing specific evidence to support your suitability for the role rather like when completing an application form.

An example layout would be:

Helen Osmond B.Sc. (Hons) 2:2

Address: 55 Arian Court
St Thomas' Drive
Any Town
Dublin   **Email:**   helen@htr-hr.co.uk

Mobile Tel: xxxxx xxxxxxxx   **Home Tel:**   0201 xxxxxxxx

Operations Manager / Commercial Manager with 10 years' experience

- **Excellent people management skills – managed 100+ staff over a 3-year period in last role**
- **Strong financial experience – worked with budgets up to €1 million**
- **Effective Strategy Manager – managed successful integration of new hardware and software systems, including introduction of major data collection changes within the business, utilising new technologies**
- **Comprehensive knowledge of Project Management with over 5 years' experience**

Project Management

Accomplished project manager with over 5 years' experience working within multifunctional teams of up to twelve staff. Recent projects include:
- IT database implementation: £30K project to implement a new state-of-the-art IT data collection and analysis system. Led a team of 6 staff.
  - Delivered the project on time and within budget
  - XXXXXXX

Summarise in the area all the project management experience you have. Remember it is important to provide a variety of examples to substantiate your ability and provide 'depth and breadth' of experience. INCLUDE achievements!

Leadership Skills

XXXXXXXXXXXXXXXXXXXXXXXXXXXXXXXXXXXXXXXXXXXXXXXXXXXXXXXXXXXXXX
XXXXXXXXXXXXXXXXXXXXXXXXXXXXXXXXXXXXXXXXXXXXXXXXXXXXXXXXXXXXXX
XXXXXXXXXX
- Xxxxxxxxx
- Xxxxxxxxxxxxxxxxxxxxxxx

Operational and Strategic Management

XXXXXXXXXXXXXXXXXXXXXXXXXXXXXXXXXXXXXXXXXXXXXXXXXXXX
XXXXXXXXXXXXXXXXXXXXXXXXXXXXXXXXXXXXXXXXXXXXXXXXX

- Xxxxxxxxxxxxxxxxxxxxxxxx
- XXXXXXXXX

EMPLOYMENT HISTORY

GFLP	2007 – 2009	Business General Manager
Dunlop Research	2001 – 2007	Project Specialist
Tri Changer	1999 – 2001	Operations Manager
J James and Sons	1983 – 1999	Programme Manager

EDUCATION AND TRAINING

1991-1992   University of Cork – BSC in Applied Sciences

Courses attended in recent years include:

Staff Motivation and Targeting; Interpersonal Managing Skills

ADDITIONAL INFORMATION

Member of the Institute of Directors
Proficient in UNIX based SPSS processing systems Quancept & Quantum

HOBBIES AND INTERESTS

Watching and playing sport, especially football and golf, travelling and reading.

Note

As already stated, it is important that these CVs are written for individual applications. If you write a skill-based CV that is not focused the CV, this can do you more harm than good. After all – as the exam question changes, so should your CV.

Functional CVs also work well for new graduates as the next sample CV demonstrates.

Helen Osmond B.Sc. (Hons) 2:2

55 Arian Court, St Thomas' Drive, Any Town, Dublin
Email: <u>helen@htr-hr.co.uk</u> **Mobile Tel:** xxxxx xxxxxxxx

Seeking a role in retail as a Trainee Retail Manager / Retail Supervisor / Retail Graduate Trainee

- **Excellent customer service and interpersonal skills having worked for over 6 months in a part-time retail role**
- **Good understanding of retail operations including: merchandising; handling payments (cash and card); dealing with deliveries / returns**
- **Able to work well under pressure and consistently deliver an excellent customer experience in busy trading periods such as Christmas**
- **Team player who is quick to learn**
- **IT proficient: Microsoft Word; Excel; PowerPoint; Access**

Customer Service Experience

Working in a customer facing role for over six months, I have learned how to relate to customers and deliver excellent customer service. For instance, whilst…(*summarise in the area all the customer service experience you have. Also, if possible, provide evidence to substantiate your ability and INCLUDE achievements!*)

Retail Skills
(A paragraph outlining your retail skills)

Interpersonal Skills
(A paragraph highlighting your interpersonal skills)

(YOU MAY HAVE 3 TO 6 SKILLS HEADINGS DEPENDING ON THE ROLE)

EMPLOYMENT HISTORY

GFLP	2012 – 2014	Retail Assistant
Dunlop Research	2011 – 2011	Temporary Admin Work

EDUCATION AND TRAINING

2015   **University of Cork – B.Sc. in Applied Sciences 2:2**

ADDITIONAL INFORMATION

Include detail as per previous CV examples

Creative CVs

Individuals from creative industries, such as: web developers; graphic designers; architects etc. can greatly enhance their CV by including samples of their drawings / work. Rather than use sketches as a watermark under your CV's content or including the diagrams within the body of the CV, we advise a cover sheet at the front of your CV.

On the cover sheet, include your name and your headline, then six samples of your work sized to be easily seen, detail clear, and chosen to demonstrate either your specialism in a specific area or your overall experience.

As an example an architectural individual may include drawings of housing designs; industrial units; schools; hospitals; refurbishments; or renovation projects. Choose these items carefully and ensure there is clarity in the drawings / sketches / diagrams. To help, label each one so a recruiter can quickly identify what they are.

For cartoonists / game designers / video and other associated creative industries, this is not so easy. In this case, place a show reel on Internet sites such as Vimeo (www.vimeo.com) and include the web link on your CV.

As an alternative, build your own website to feature your productions. One company we recommend to host a website is 1&1 (www.1and1.com in Ireland and for the UK www.1and1.co.uk). They provide cheap web hosting and excellent website templates.

Academic CVs

Those looking for academic roles are often asked to provide a CV with a covering letter when applying. If you are looking at these roles, please IGNORE all the advice we have provided with regard to CV layout, structure, and including CV bullet points / headlines / personal statements.

Yes – ignore …

Academic CVs are based upon a CV format that has not changed over the last 30 years, if not longer. Education is featured at the top of the CV, areas of research often next, and at the end of the CV publications and patients. Somewhere in the middle, career history is featured.

If you are looking at roles in this sector, we can email you a sample CV. Please contact us via our email address featured on our website.

For you, the most important part of your application is your covering letter, as it is used to highlight your suitability for the academic research or teaching role.

Phrases and words for CVs

The language used in a CV can really help to 'sell' you and project a certain image. For instance, "Performance-managed twenty staff…" sounds far more impressive than "Managed twenty staff…" Here are some words that can be incorporated into your CV to emphasise your abilities:

Accountable	Achieved	Adaptable	Ambitious
Analytical	Articulate	Capable	Challenging
Committed	Competitive	Concise	Confident
Conscientious	Consistent	Consultative	Creative
Decisive	Dedicated	Determined	Diplomatic
Efficient	Empowering	Entrepreneurial	Enthusiastic
Fair	Flexible	Friendly	Genuine
Helpful	Honest	Imaginative	Independent
Influential	Innovative	Inspirational	Inventive
Knowledgeable	Logical	Loyal	Motivational
Objective	Optimistic	Organised	Originate
Perceptive	Perfectionist	Persistent	Persuasive
Pioneering	Positive	Practical	Pragmatic
Precise	Professional	Proactive	Performance
Realistic	Reconcile	Reliable	Resolved
Resourceful	Responsible	Risk	Scientific
Self-Reliant	Shaped	Sincere	Supportive
Systematic	Thoughtful	Tolerant	Tenacious
Versatile	Visionary		

When highlighting achievements, by starting the achievement with an 'action' word you can emphasise the achievement. Words such as:

Accomplished	Attained	Achieved	Analysed
Created	Calculated	Consolidated	Conceived
Conducted	Converted	Designed	Directed
Defined	Developed	Ensured	Established
Engineered	Eradicated	Exceeded	Expanded
Enhanced	Executed	Evaluated	Founded
Generated	Headed	Halved	Highlighted
Instigated	Introduced	Inspired	Initiated
Led	Launched	Liaise	Lowered
Met	Modified	Minimised	Motivated
Negotiated	Originated	Overcame	Outlined
Organised	Optimised	Performance	Piloted
Performed	Proposed	Promoted	Reorganised
Restructured	Revamped	Recommended	Resolved
Retained	Specified	Shaped	Saved
Streamlined	Strengthened	Set up	Solved
Scheduled	Stimulated	Supported	Transformed

Application forms

CVs tend to often allude to a skill and tend to be brief overviews of your abilities and capabilities. Application forms are the opposite, asking you to provide lots of detail and often examples to demonstrate your ability and experience in an area.

The first thing to note is that, when filling application forms in, read the instructions and follow them precisely. If it says use a black pen, use a black pen or you might just be rejected for the colour of the ink – it does happen.

Print clearly, use a dictionary, and if online, try to print the form off before completing it, giving you time to think about what you are going to type in.

So how do you fill them in?

The majority of the form is usually simple to complete, asking for personal, employment and educational details. The most important area is where you are asked to provide supporting evidence.

If the application form has a number of individual boxes to fill in, read the question carefully and enter evidence into each. Most application forms have one large empty supporting evidence box, so when completing it:

1. Use the person specification as the basis for your statement
2. Treat each point on the person specification as a separate exam question
3. Highlight each point in turn in the supporting evidence box – you can even copy the language from the specification over
4. Now provide an overview of how you met the requirement; next specific detail; and potentially examples to help provide depth and support your application

If you are asked to use additional sheets as required, often they expect this. This box may be scored like an exam. If not enough evidence = lower score.

One way to gain extra marks is to provide examples to support your application, and when recounting these examples we suggest using the S.T.A.R. technique as it will help to structure your evidence:

S = Situation – Describe the scene and this MUST be done well
T = Tasks – Identify any tasks involved and their importance
A = Actions – Your actions
R = Results – The benefit/results you achieved

Too many people do just an **A.R**… but setting the scene is critical to be judged properly. Ideally, then, think of the example you provide being marked and include detail to gain the marks:

Situation / Task (often combined)	4 marks
Actions you took	4 marks
Results	2 marks

(A variation on this is **I.P.A.R.**   I=Introduction; **P**=Problem; **A**=Action; **R**=Results)

© Job Doctor

Effective job hunting - build a job search action plan

How we look for a new job has changed drastically in recent years. No longer are jobs in local papers, nor are Recruitment Agencies filling 40% of jobs as they did back in the 1990s.

There have been many surveys on where people find a new job – as a rough guide, the breakdown currently is thought to be:

- Press and Trade magazine advertising   2%
- Agencies   5%
- Internet (Job Boards / CV Databases)   60%
- Networking (contacts, friends, etc.)   15%
- Speculative Approaches   15%

As you can see, the focus of job hunting is now very much on using online tools.

You are about to be guided through a structured approach to job hunting which will help you produce a personal action plan of activities. Before we start, there are a few basic tips to remember:

- Write a CV focused upon a job type / role
- Tailor your CV to the role if applying for a specific job
- Tailor your covering letter to each job applied for

Remember that the survey in 'The Times' stated that a teenager's CV is screened by recruiters in an 8.8-second 'first sift'. Over 19 years of age this rises to 15 to 30 seconds, so quality applications have more impact than unfocused ones.

A few other areas to consider are:

Internet access

If you do not have Internet access at home, remember that Public Libraries provide access. If you have a laptop, tablet or smartphone with a wireless connection, you can also get free Internet access at McDonalds, Tesco, Marks & Spencer and Costa Coffee.

Set up an email account – check your spam box

When applying for most jobs, you will be asked to email your CV. It is important therefore, to set up a personal email account that is checked daily. If you do not have one, you can open up a free email account with Yahoo, Hotmail or Gmail.

It is also important to check your spam or junk mailbox on a daily basis. Recruiters often use email as a first means of contact, and for unknown reasons it is not uncommon that their emails end up not in your inbox, but in your spam or junk mailbox.

When looking for a new job, a mobile phone is essential. An interviewer will ring a mobile phone to contact a person about a job in preference to writing to them or ringing a home number.

If you do not have a mobile phone, ask a family member who has one to take calls for you.

Ensure that it is switched on at all times and the voicemail is turned on. Also ensure any recorded message is appropriate and not silly.

Identity fraud protection

A key thing to take into consideration is identity fraud protection. When you upload your CV to a website, you assume it is safe and access to it is carefully restricted. In reality, although we are about to recommend uploading your CV to CV databases, these do get hacked into by fraudsters.

So we recommend you have two CVs: one with all your details on it; the other with reduced personal information that you upload to the CV databases. Changes on the second CV may include removing:

- Address, highlight the area you live in: 'Home Location – Dublin'
- Date of Birth, if you want your age on it: 'Age – 35 years'
- Home Telephone Number, but include your mobile number
- Marital Status / Maiden Name
- Names of schools or colleges attended but leave on exams passed
- Details of any Local Clubs or Associations
- Current employer's name – merely describe their business

Your full CV can be forwarded when you know who will be reading it.

Structured action plan

It is also important that you use all the tools available in your job hunt relevant to your own situation. We will now guide you through the main job search tools helping to formulate a structured action plan.

CV databases

CV databases are large databases of CVs that job boards have built up over recent years. Access to the database is sold to both recruitment agencies and employers.

In the UK they contain millions of CVs, with CV Library currently having over 11 million CVs on its database; Monster is estimated to have over 15 million CVs on their UK site. In Ireland, with its smaller population, the figures are significantly smaller, but their use by employers is growing.

This history behind them is that as job boards became more established, instead of merely listing job adverts they started to ask you to upload your CV to their website; the site then forwards your CV onto the recruiter. As the databases grew, the owners of the sites started to sell access to recruitment agencies, and then employers. In the same way you can search for a new TV on Google, recruiters can search a CV database and within seconds identify candidates for a job.

Estimates are that they are now used by recruiters to fill at least 50% of jobs in some sectors, so a key part of job hunting is to upload your CV to these CV databases – but which ones?

Industry-specific / specialist CV databases

When looking for CV databases to put your CV onto try and identify industry-specific job boards. There are some websites that only advertise engineering jobs, sales jobs, finance jobs etc. Attached to these job boards are CV databases. If the job board only advertises sales roles, the database will be full of CVs of people looking for sales jobs.

So one option a recruiter has when looking to fill a sales job is to buy access to these specialist boards rather than the more general job boards. Although often smaller databases, they are cheaper to purchase access to and – if all you want is a sales person – potentially as effective at identifying candidates.

The best way to identify the industry-specific sites is to carry out a search on a search engine such as Google, Yahoo or Bing.

Simply type in phrases such as:

'IT jobs'	'Secretarial jobs'	'Project manager jobs'
'Engineering jobs'	'Teaching jobs'	

Follow the numerous links in the search results and upload your CV to the relevant job boards.

You may need to broaden how you search, for instance if looking for e.g. a role in purchasing, search under:

'Purchasing jobs' and 'Buying jobs' and 'Procurement jobs'

Likewise for accountancy jobs:

'Accountancy jobs' and 'Finance jobs'

Unlike most searches, where you may merely look at pages one and two of the results, we recommend going at least five pages down. Mixed in with the results will be recruitment agencies that may also be worth contacting. As you see likely job boards, look for the 'Upload your CV' link and do just that; opening accounts on the websites is free although in the past some job boards such as The Ladders did charge a fee (now only trading in the USA).

Interim job boards

If you are looking for interim or contract positions, it is worth searching under the term 'interim jobs'. One of the main interim job boards covering both the UK and Ireland is: www.interimmanagementjobs.net

Executive job boards

For more senior roles, search for 'executive jobs' or 'director jobs'.

However, do not place your CV on these sites alone if looking for a senior role; industry-specific websites will also advertise senior roles.

Senior vacancy sites covering both the UK and Ireland:

www.exec-appointments.com   www.executivesontheweb.com

Main job boards

Now you have placed your CV on the specialist boards, you need to upload it to the major job boards that cover most, if not quite all, job roles. These are promoted actively to employers and employment agencies, and are often the first point of call when a vacancy arises.

The ones we would recommend you MUST place your CV on are:

UK–wide:

www.fish4jobs.co.uk   www.reed.co.uk
www.monster.co.uk   www.totaljobs.co.uk
www.jobsite.co.uk   www.cv-library.co.uk
www.indeed.co.uk

Scotland:
www.scotcareers.co.uk   www.s1jobs.com

Northern Ireland:
www.NIjobs.com

Ireland:

www.jobs.ie   www.irishjobs.ie
www.indeed.ie   www.monster.ie
www.cv-library.co.uk

National press boards

Traditionally some jobs were advertised in the national press and they still advertise such roles in Sunday supplements etc., so you may also want to consider in the UK:

http://jobs.guardian.co.uk   http://jobs.timesonline.co.uk

In Ireland, the Irish Times now lets you upload a copy of your CV to their database:

www.irishtimes.com

Regional and local newspaper boards

Now, if you are a local employer and looking to recruit a local person to fill a role, you may decide to buy in a CV database operated by a local job board.

Smaller in size and cheaper to purchase than the national CV databases, they will only have people looking for work in the local area, so also carry out a search for jobs in your local town or region on Google and upload your CV to these local job boards. Many are operated by local papers and, for example, a search for 'Jobs in London' would identify:

www.londonjobs.co.uk

Other regional sites include:

www.mymanchesterjobs.co.uk   www.mywestmidlandsjobs.co.uk

Ireland has local boards specific to a region, such as Dublin (www.dublinjobs.ie) and Cork (www.corkjobs.ie), and recently the option to add your CV to their CV database was added – powered by CV-library.

Graduate boards

If looking for graduate training schemes or entry-level roles, a further search would be 'Graduate Jobs'. Sites to upload your CV to include:

www.gradjobs.co.uk   www.graduate-jobs.com
www.targetjobs.co.uk   www.milkround.com

These sites should also be visited for graduates looking for work in Ireland, with many international companies using them to fill graduate positions.

Company job boards

Some companies, such as Kellogg's, have invested in CV database software for themselves. On the company's website you are presented with the opportunity to add your details to their CV database, which is then searched by their staff as vacancies arise. Therefore, if you have an interest in working for a specific employer, visit their site and upload your CV.

A site that is very popular in the UK is the NHS: www.jobs.nhs.uk

UK Universal job match – Jobcentre plus

The final CV database you may want to upload your CV to in the UK is run by Jobcentre Plus: Universal Job Match. If registered as unemployed, you will be required to use this site for job hunting and to upload a copy of your CV.

   www.gov.uk/jobsearch

How to upload your CV

When you visit a job board, there will be an option to 'Upload your CV' or 'create a profile'. Often there is a link saying 'Get headhunted – let employers find you'.

To upload your CV, follow these links and fill in the fields as required. At some point you will be asked to upload your CV and this will involve finding it on your computer, selecting it, and then hitting the upload button. Your email address is used as your log-in.

When you upload your CV to the job sites, make sure you select the option to add your CV to the searchable CV database. Some sites, such as CV Library, will automatically add your CV to the database sold to recruiters, but many other sites do not, keeping it private and you need to select this option.

Uploading several CVs to the searchable databases

If you are looking for two or more differing roles, you may have several CVs that you would like to add to the searchable CV database. Some websites allow you to upload several CVs to apply for jobs with, but only one CV can be added to the searchable database. The way to get around this is to open multiple accounts by creating several email addresses; by having two email addresses, you can upload CV one on email address one, CV two on email address two etc.

Refresh your CV weekly

A common mistake people make when using CV databases is that they upload their CV and expect it to be found by recruiters after several months. One search field a recruiter can use to narrow down their search is by how old the CV is.

Being practical if a database has 10 million CVs on it, approximately 1 in 5 of the UK working population, would you search for CVs more than one month old?

Most recruiters are looking for 20 or 30 CVs to screen, not 300, and will initially search CVs less than 7 days old. If they only find 5 candidates, they will then extend the search accordingly.

So, if your CV is over one week old, it may not be found in searches; it is important to refresh your CV once a week.

To refresh your CV, you do not need to change anything on it – merely re-upload it to replace the CV stored on the database. If the site imports your CV into sections such as Education or Employment History, click to edit a section and then save the section again without changing it.

The best time to refresh your CV is Sunday due to another feature of CV databases: recruiter CV alerts.

Recruiter CV alerts

Recruiters searching the databases for candidates have the option to save their search as a CV alert. Every time a CV is refreshed or uploaded it is compared to the saved search, and if a match is found, the CV is emailed to the recruiter.

So, by refreshing your CV weekly, not only will it hopefully appear in recruiters' searches, it will also be emailed out to recruiters searching for your precise skills.

The CVs are emailed out to recruiters in the early hours of the morning following the day you uploaded or refreshed your CV. Most people put aside time on a Monday to read the emails they received over the weekend. By refreshing your CV on the Sunday, it will be at the top of the recruiter's inbox on Monday morning, so hopefully read first.

Looking to work abroad? Finding international job boards

For those looking to work abroad, the trick is to search for job boards on country-specific search engine and upload your CV to the local job boards.

If using Google to search international versions, include:

Germany	www.google.de	France	www.google.fr
Spain	www.google.es	Australia	www.google.com.au

Be found in CV database searches

A final point to note is that, in addition to refreshing your CV so it is found in searches, you must also include on the CV generic job titles and job title variations.

A recruiter searching for a Finance Assistant would enter that precise term or potentially:

Accounts Assistant OR Purchase Ledger Clerk OR Accounts Clerk

They may refine their search further by adding in 'Sage Line 50' (an accountancy IT package), so ensure you also have a variety of relevant buzz words on your CV.

Students / career changers

As mentioned earlier in this guide, if you are a recent student or looking to move into a new employment area, you need to include on your CV job titles of roles you would like to do. This can be achieved by using a statement such as:

'Seeking a role as a Finance Assistant or Accounts Clerk'

Without the job titles on your CV you will not be found by recruiters in their searches.

Stopping your employer finding your CV

Many employers who purchase access to a CV database will set up permanent CV alerts to inform them when a CV is placed on a database with their company name on it.

Why? Well, to see if any of their staff are looking for alternative employment... not always a good thing to advertise to your employer.

To help prevent your CV your appearing in these CV alerts, some sites try to block this employer search, while others offer you a privacy option. The privacy option does not always work effectively, so if you are currently employed, we suggest removing your current employer's name from your CV along with your surname.

CV database – view the search screen

If you would like to see how a recruiter searches a CV database, CV Library has a test search screen that can be viewed.

First, go to the home page at www.cv-library.co.uk and on the right hand side of the screen halfway down, click on the tab named 'Recruiting?'

In the centre it has a section named: 'Search our CV database' and underneath 'Start searching CVs'. Select 'Start Searching CVs'.

On the next screen, select 'Test Search'.

Local papers / trade magazines

The use of newspapers or trade magazines to advertise jobs has declined over recent years in favour of online job boards, although they still tend to feature public sector jobs. What they now provide is an excellent resource tool, giving you leads and information for speculative applications:

- Local employers (often featured in the business pages)
- Agencies who may specialise in your chosen field

But as far as using them for job hunting is concerned, few if any jobs will be in them.

Jobcentre Plus (UK) & Department of Social Protection (Ireland)

Jobcentre Plus

Jobcentre Plus states that up to 30% of jobs are advertised with them; a third of those are management, technical or professional.

A past UK government incentivised employers to take candidates from the job centres by providing a £1,000 employer bonus (golden hello) and a £1,500 training allowance for every person employed. This drove employers to the job centres and, although the incentives have gone, many employers are still placing all their vacancies with them.

> www.gov.uk/jobsearch
> www.jobcentreonline.com (Northern Ireland)

The Department of Social Protection

In Ireland after the liquidation of FAS, the Department of Social Protection has taken over running the government-owned job board. This site advertises roles at almost all levels and is an excellent job board. In addition to advertising jobs, the site provides details on training, internships and other job seeker resources. The job search engine can be accessed from the home page:

> www.welfare.ie

Job board 'job alerts'

From your searches to identify CV databases to add your CV to, you will have a list of job boards where jobs are also advertised. After you have searched these sites for potential roles, one option you have after your search is to save your job search as a job alert. This is sometimes referred to as 'jobs by email'.

Rather than visit the site daily, the site will email you daily relevant jobs based upon your search criteria.

<u>Boolean language</u>

When searching individual job boards, we suggest you learn how to use Boolean language. You can use this to effectively refine your searches.

If you search for a role as: Administration Manager, by placing words in speech marks the search will be for the exact phrase: "Administration Manager". Without the " ", results will feature jobs adverts that include both words but they may be separate and not together as in a job title.

The search can further be refined by the use of 'AND', 'OR' and 'NOT'

"Administration Manager" OR "General Manager"

For most people, however, we do not recommend setting up these individual job alerts or searching the individual job boards for vacancies, instead using the job search meta-crawlers or search engines.

Job board search engines / meta-crawlers / job crawlers

In recent years, search engines have been set up that search numerous job boards.

The main UK ones are:

- www.indeed.co.uk
- www.workhound.co.uk
- www.jobrapido.co.uk
- www.simplyhired.co.uk

In Ireland, we recommend:

- www.indeed.ie
- www.careerjet.ie
- www.simplehired.ie

The big advantage of the search engines is that they search:

- Industry-specific job boards
- Regional job boards
- National job boards
- Executive job boards
- Graduate job boards
- Interim job boards
- Recruitment agency job boards

- Employers' job boards
- National and local government job boards
- The NHS job board in the UK
- Jobcentre Plus and The Department of Social Protection job boards
- Almost everywhere jobs can be advertised online...

The one search engine we tend to recommend most is Indeed, purely because there is an advanced search option that helps to refine your searches easily. The advanced search link is just to the right and under the 'Where' box on the home page. Indeed is also free to use.

Using the advanced search, you can search under a range of criteria. In addition, you can remove irrelevant job roles from the search results by using negative search terms.

It is worth spending time refining your search and, when done, Indeed also allows you to set up daily job alerts by entering your email address into the 'Get new jobs for this search by email' box on the search results page.

If you set up these alerts, the site will initially ask you to confirm your email address and set up a password.

Like any other search engine, Indeed will feature in the search results links that go to the job boards where the jobs are advertised. When you follow these links, it may then be necessary to set up an account in order to apply for the job of interest.

More recently, Indeed has expanded the services it offers and now includes the option to upload your CV to their CV database; it also has its own job board.

Note – In the past jobs advertised on the job board of LinkedIn would appear in the search results of many of these search engines. More recently we are finding their jobs not all appearing in the search engine results. So although you can rely upon Indeed to bring in vacancy details off numerous job boards, set up a separate job search alert on LinkedIn to be certain not to miss potential vacancies – covered later.

Use the search engines to search employer job boards

Employers are discovering that jobs featured on their own company websites are now being listed in the search engines. Many, as a result, have stopped advertising on commercial job boards, saving them thousands of pounds / euros in advertising fees.

The number of applicants may be less, but with people increasingly understanding how to use sites like Indeed, the employers are attracting relevant candidates.

From a job seeker's point of view this is of great benefit, with fewer people applying to employer website advertised roles.

Use the search engines to apply to very fresh jobs

Most people set up job alerts that arrive the morning of the day after the job advert was uploaded. If you want to get the jump on other applicants, Indeed can help you in another way. You must be on the same device or computer for this to work.

Start by carrying out an initial search and setting up a job alert.

After a few hours, log back into Indeed and you will see previous searches listed at the bottom of the page. It takes a few hours to start to work properly, but indeed is continually scouring the web for new job adverts and you will often see beside the previous search that it has identified some new jobs for you:

"finance assistant" £15,000+ Manchester – 15 new (UK)

"finance assistant" €15,000+ Dublin – 15 new (Ireland)

By following these links, you will see what can often be very fresh and newly uploaded jobs. The time to log in is late morning around 11.30am and late afternoon around 3.45pm. If you are lucky you will see jobs that are 1 hour old, 12 minutes old etc.

Now imagine the recruiter uploaded a job one hour ago – your CV is one of the first to arrive and it highlights that you are potentially a good candidate. Would the recruiter wait until the next day to see who else sends in their CV or might they ring you and ask you down for an interview?

This really does work! We helped one individual gain a job in less than 23 hours by doing just that…

International job search engines

If looking for work abroad, the search engine to use is Jobrapido as it has nearly 60 international versions of their search engine. To find them, log into your local site – either www.jobrapido.co.uk or www.jobrapido.ie – then click on the country logo at the top to select the country search engine you are looking for.

Indeed also has a number of international search engines, but these are harder to find. It may be worth finding out the usual country website ending, such as .fr for France or .es for Spain, then adding them onto Indeed and trying the website address. For instance: www.indeed.es works for Spain; www.indeed.fr for France.

Search effectively

When searching for jobs, what you must consider is that employers may use different job titles to describe the same role:

Programmer = Software Technician = Software Developer = ???
Operations Manager = General Manager = Office Manager = ???

This means you need to widen your searches to include job title variations and possibly set up several job alerts.

Another way to search is under a specific word. In finance they use ledgers, so rather than set up searches for 'Accounts Clerk' or 'Finance Assistant' and the numerous variations of job title, set up an alert for 'ledger'. Searching under specific jargon or buzz words can be far more effective for identifying potential jobs to apply for.

Recruitment agencies

Recruitment agencies / job agencies generate their income from placing people into jobs by charging a placement fee to the company that employs them. Their fees range from 15% to 30% of the successful recruit's annual salary.

Although filling far fewer jobs in recent years, they are a valuable tool to use and in sectors such as IT and Finance they are still dominant, filling up to 50% of jobs in those fields, although overall they only fill approx. 5% of jobs.

Recruitment consultants are fundamentally sales people; most agencies will have their consultants ringing companies trying to identify vacancies between 10am and midday, and 2pm and 4pm. If you ring the agency between these times it is unlikely you will be able to speak to the consultant, although receptionists are usually primed to take down your details and record the fact that you have rung, thus identifying you are still actively looking for work.

You may be used to seeing large agencies such as Reed or Manpower on the high street, but there will often be numerous other agencies in a town or city. To find them, look online at sites such as Yell (UK) and White Pages (Ireland) by searching under Recruitment Agencies.

The majority of vacancies you see advertised by an agency will either be vacancies they cannot fill or ones that are termed 'bread and butter' positions. If you see an advertised job in your field, but feel it may not be quite right for you, send them your CV anyway as they may have other vacancies on their books that are ideal for your experience and skills.

> **What you must remember is that agencies are there to fill vacancies, NOT to find you a job…**

As far as the consultants are concerned, most really do not care which candidate gets the job as long as it is one of their candidates that does. This means you risk being one of many unless you have rare skills, but there are techniques to get them on your side and working for you.

The basic principle is to work on your relationship with the agency consultant in order to build a rapport that will ensure you are high-profile to them.

But how can you achieve this?

- Where possible, go and register with the consultant in person
- Phone the consultant weekly or fortnightly so they do not forget you. THIS IS THE MOST IMPORTANT THING TO DO… do not pester them, but keep in regular contact or you will be forgotten…!
- If the agency is local, drop in occasionally, even if you only get to speak to the receptionist – you will keep the contact going
- If you register your CV by post or email, phone the consultant a few days later to discuss what possible vacancies they may have
- If you register by email, re-submit the CV every 3 months and mention that it has been updated (even if unaltered). Most agencies will archive your CV after 3 months, assuming you have found alternative employment

Other things to consider:

- Treat the consultant with respect
- Register with a number of agencies in your field. Companies will often have preferred agencies or long-standing relationships with only one or two agencies. If you register with only one agency, you are severely limiting your employment prospects.
- Register with industry-specific agencies, which may be at the other end of the country, but who operate nationally

The main thing is to keep in regular contact with them by ringing them weekly or fortnightly.

Independent recruiters

In 2009 a large number of recruitment consultants were made redundant as the recession hit and many went self-employed. Working from home, they run successful businesses and it is often the independent recruiter who can be of most use in your job search.

How do you find them? Very difficult – they tend to find you. By uploading your CV to the databases, they can find it and ring you about job roles. Do not be surprised if, when they ask to meet up, you end up in a Costa Coffee or even the café in a Tesco Extra – many of them work from home offices.

Temporary work / contract / interim positions

One last thing to note is that agencies nowadays supply larger companies with temporary staff on a long-term basis; companies such as IBM for all their administration and non-IT-specific roles. Do not ignore this as an option.

If you would consider contract or temporary work, agencies often have different consultants handling these roles, so make sure you are registered with both.

> **WARNING** – When you register with an agency, you will often be asked by the consultant for a list of companies your details have been put forward to already, 'so we do not end up sending in your details twice and wasting time'.
>
> This is, on the whole, untrue and what they are really trying to do is identify companies with vacancies to fill that are on other agencies' books. If you provide such a list, they are likely to be on the phone canvassing them and putting their candidates forward. You are creating competition for yourself and we recommend that you do not provide this information.

Students and returners to work

If you are starting out in your career or returning to employment after a career break, temporary work is an ideal way of getting practical work experience on your CV.

Graduates may also find recruitment agencies a good way of gaining graduate entry-level positions. For instance, law firms are increasingly asking agencies to recruit newly-qualified law graduates for them as paralegals, with the intention of offering good recruits the opportunity of moving onto a training contract to become a qualified solicitor at a later date.

In addition, if you are looking to become a teacher in the UK, teaching agencies are actively encouraged by the UK government to recruit new graduates as teaching assistants with a view to training them up as teachers. This is to help them gain 12 months' school-based experience before being allowed onto a teacher training course.

Networking

Networking is exactly what it says: talking to people you know and letting them know you are looking for a new job – friends, family, former clients, people you met at trade exhibitions or ex-colleagues.

In the days before the Internet, approximately 25% of people achieved employment this way.

Ex-colleagues can be an excellent source of leads for potential vacancies, possibly passing your details onto their new employer.

Also, if being made redundant with others, keep in touch with your ex-colleagues; they may be approached about a role that was not suitable for them, but perfect for you. By staying in contact, they can pass across leads for jobs.

Another way of networking is by joining a trade body, where a lot of contacts can be generated in a very short time.

Friends and family can also be an invaluable source of job leads.

A useful site to help with networking is LinkedIn (www.linkedin.com).

Note – The people you know are often not the people who get you a job – it is their contacts, and you should use them as a link.

LinkedIn

LinkedIn was established originally as a networking site for professionals and executives. It is now used by individuals at all levels.

To a lot of recruiters, LinkedIn (www.linkedin.com) is a free CV database. Using Boolean language, they search in the top search field under job titles, skills, location and potentially qualifications. In the search results they can view profiles of potential candidates. This means a profile on LinkedIn is essential for all job hunters.

LinkedIn is also now actively promoted as a CV database and many recruiters purchase the search engine facility, allowing them total access to profiles.

Joining the site is free, and as you sign up you are provided with the option to email everyone in your address book an invitation to connect with you on the site.

Profile

Once your account is open, you create a profile for yourself. This is in effect a very public copy of your CV, so think carefully about the detail you provide and remember identity fraud implications. We recommend not placing your date of birth on the site anywhere.

Summary

The most important part of your profile is your summary, which should include some solid facts about yourself and what you can offer a potential employer. For graduates and those looking for entry level positions, or to return to employment, use the summary to advertise the fact you are 'seeking a role as a...', but be careful not to make this too general as it may highlight to a potential employer a lack of clear career direction.

Include in your summary some soft skills such as 'good team player', but too many fluffy unsubstantiated words will lose your profile's impact. To help strengthen your summary, think about including some of your achievements. This will help highlight how good you are as a potential employee.

Using the CV-writing technique of including a headline on your CV with 6 to 8 bullet points underneath, covered earlier in the CV writing section, it means writing your summary becomes very easy. All you will need to do is copy the bullet points from your CV into the summary section and use them as a basis for your summary, possibly turning them into sentences.

Skills section

Another important section is the 'Skills Section'. This is where you are asked to list your skills as buzz words and phrases. The skills section appears towards the bottom of the profile and should be viewed as a list of potential search terms a recruiter may use to find you in the search engine. As you start to type in a word, the site auto-suggests words and phrases for you. Spend time on this section to get the right key words. Later on you may see people endorse you for the skills you enter, but for job hunters it is about listing the skills recruiters could search under and not about getting the endorsements.

Ask for recommendations

Another key thing to obtain is recommendations from your old boss or colleagues. These are where the person writes, in effect, an online reference that you post onto your profile. With employer references often only stating your name, job title and dates of employment in a reference nowadays, this online recommendation from a key individual may impress a recruiter reviewing your profile as part of the selection process – yes, recruiters are increasingly looking at your profile as part of the screening process.

Job role details

As regards providing a lot of detail under job roles, this is not actually necessary if you have a well-written summary.

Link to people

Next, you need to link to people you know. Linking to people is important as it allows greater access to your profile. Recruiters purchasing LinkedIn as a CV database will have access to your profile, but those using it as a free way of recruiting can only view your profile if you are a 1st, 2nd or 3rd connection (2nd level connections are people your contacts know; 3rd people those contacts know).

You can, as mentioned, allow the site to email all your contacts in your electronic address book, but it might be best to be more selective and track down people you know using the search engine on the website.

LinkedIn as a CV database – make sure you are found

There are several tricks to making sure your profile is found by potential recruiters, especially the ones not paying for the site:

- Make your profile very accessible by linking to people you know. It is not them who might be searching for the profile, but recruiters who may be 2nd or even 3rd level contacts
- Recruiters search using Boolean language and, just like on your CV, it is important to include generic job titles and buzz words in your profile if they are not listed in your skills section

- List your current role as being 'Seeking new opportunity' or 'Seeking new role'. Obviously do not do this if you are still employed...! Alternatively, include the phrase in your summary. The important word to include is 'seeking', used by recruiters to narrow down a profile search. Seeking tends to appear in job hunters' profiles as it sounds far better than 'looking for a job'.
- Adjust your security settings to allow your email address to be viewed by people finding your profile
- Join 'Groups'. Groups are set up to represent a sector and are often industry-related. By joining a group, you can post comments to topical subjects that will improve your profile. LinkedIn will often let group members view each other's profiles (although not always) and contact them directly, so again you are increasing your visibility. You can join up to 50 groups and even if you do not participate in conversations, you can use your membership to network with other members or make speculative approaches to potential employer contacts
- Add locations where you would like to work to your summary. This is to help recruiters searching for free who have restricted their search scope. They will tend to search under locations such as Glasgow and unless your profile includes Glasgow in it as where you live, have worked or went to university, you will not appear in their search results. Simply add to your profile a phrase such as: 'currently seeking employment in the following areas: Glasgow, Linlithgow, Edinburgh'.

Finally there is then the option to upgrade your membership to a Premium Account at a cost. This allows anyone finding your profile to view it in full.

LinkedIn job board

LinkedIn is now actively promoting itself as a job board to employers. They have recently introduced a 'job app' to further develop their position as a job board as well as a networking site, CV database, etc.

Jobs advertised on LinkedIn as mentioned earlier used to appear in the search results of the job search engines such as Indeed, but recently we have found not all their jobs appearing. We recommend therefore a separate job alert is set up on LinkedIn to complement the search results of Indeed etc.

Other uses of LinkedIn

In addition to being a CV database, LinkedIn can help you:

- Track down ex-colleagues and contact them via the site
- Research your interviewer
- For speculative approaches, it can help you identify named contacts within target businesses for you to approach. You can even contact them via the site, asking them to connect to you. If doing this, select the 'Friend' option as to how you know them or the site will block the approach.

- Create a positive profile on yourself that interviewers will often reference as part of the selection technique
- Keep in contact with ex-colleagues also made redundant, who may have information that can help you find a job as they carry out their own job hunt
- Use the site to gain introductions by asking people to connect to you, and then engaging in conversations with them
- Send updates to your network to update your status
- Keep on recruiters' radars. For those who are made redundant and were head-hunted whilst employed, LinkedIn keeps you contactable. After you left your old company, did you tell everyone your new mobile number?
- If starting your own business, you can create a company LinkedIn page (FOC). This is especially useful also if looking for interim or contract / freelance roles.
- Advertise your new business via the site (cost involved)
- Help your own website ranking on Google and other search engines. Your activity on sites such as LinkedIn helps with your site ranking, so by posting articles on a company page you will get Google brownie points.
- As the site evolves… the list only keeps growing

Speculative approaches

The basic principle of speculative approaches is that, on average, an employer will have between 10% and 35% staff turnover each year. By sending in a speculative copy of your CV, you may just have perfect timing and be asked in for an interview or kept on file for future jobs. Companies retain CVs as they offer fee-free recruitment.

So where do you find details of who to send your CV to?

- Search on Google etc. If your field is Electronics, key in 'electronics companies' to find a list of electronics companies.
- Look on Yell / White Pages and search for competitors by using their industry classifications or by searching industry sectors
- Search also by area
- If you have specific qualifications such as 'Six Sigma', search for press releases from companies using it
- Ask your sales force who your competitors are
- Walk or drive around an area compiling a list of employers
- Use LinkedIn to identify named contacts

So you have your list – now what? Rather than post a CV addressed 'To whom it may concern', ring the company and ask for the name of the relevant person likely to employ you.

A named approach is far more fruitful. If possible, obtain an email address to utilise for ease and speed.

The line manager is often the decision maker in the recruitment process, with the Human Resources team only there to offer advice and support the process. It is better in the first instance to send your CV to the line manager or even the chief executive, although you may end up being referred to HR anyway.

When trying to find out who to send your CV, to one problem often encountered is that a lot of companies have a policy not to give out names of line managers. To get around this, either use LinkedIn to identify named individuals in the organisation or ask for the managing director's PA as switchboards will often put you through to them even if you don't know the MD's name.

When you apply, remember to include a simple covering letter / email with your CV stating what type of work you are looking for and highlighting your skills and experience. One page is enough for a covering letter, and we suggest you follow up with a telephone call a week or so later.

Try to not to state job roles in your letter as this will narrow down how the person receiving your application will view you, and thus roles they might consider you for. Instead, highlight areas you could work in such as Finance; Sales; Customer Service.

Finally, resubmit your CV after 3 months to make sure they still have you on file.

Direct 'walk-in' approaches

Another form of speculative approach is the walk-in. It is what it says – you take the direct approach of walking around an area, calling into companies and dropping a copy of your CV off with relevant individuals in person.

This can be highly effective, as with an Accountant we supported walking into a number of local practices, asked for the managing partner and gaining a 6-month temporary contract as a result.

You may not always get to see the person you need, so write a brief note to go with your CV and take envelopes with you. When the individual is not available to come out to see you, place your CV within the envelope and with the covering letter. Write on the front the person's name and seal the envelope. Then ask for it to be passed to them. By doing so you stop the whole company reading your CV before it reaches the line manager.

Social media

Social media is being increasingly used by companies to both promote their products and services and in recent years it is increasingly being used to attract new employees.

In the 2015 National Recruiters Survey, 92% of employers stated they were using social media as part of their recruitment strategy. This may be as simple as placing job advertisements on their own social media, but many are utilising it more fully. The survey also highlighted that:

- 87% are using LinkedIn
- 55% are using Facebook
- 47% are using Twitter

Recruiters aren't afraid of new platforms either, with three percent using Snapchat during their process, as well as small forays into Vimeo, Tumblr and Periscope. Social media needs therefore to be part of any job hunter's strategy.

Facebook launched in 2003 and at the end of 2015 there were 1,591 billion monthly users, and employers are tapping into this pool of people to fill jobs.

Following potential employers on social media

Company social media activity is often used to promote a business with the intention of driving traffic to their website. Featuring company profiles on social media they include information about the company, news and latest updates on products or services, many hoping to gain social media followers.

To help build up a following companies will often via social media comment on topical issues. A Law firm dealing with employment law may comment on new legislation, by posting engaging information rather than merely projecting their company products or services.

Having built up this following, recruiters advertise new jobs to their followers. So, if you are keen to work for an organisation one recommendation is to start to follow them on Twitter or LinkedIn to receive job updates, although it must be said that these vacancies will be also found via other channels. If you are not interested in the organisation the updates can be slightly annoying.

What is noticeably being seen though is more sophisticated use of social media to attract talent. Companies recruiting highly specialist roles are using social media actively to gain followers by hosting topical conversations and then actively searching within their followers and headhunting from them; so, if this is you, think about following the competitors to your own employer / ex-employer even if you are not interested in their general posts or Tweets.

Jobs advertised on social media – you will need an account to see them

LinkedIn has its own job board as mentioned in an earlier section, and employers are increasingly advertising roles on LinkedIn in preference to more traditional job boards such as Monster, Reed, or Fish4jobs. As a job hunter, to see these roles you will need to open accounts on LinkedIn, Facebook etc.

Facebook posts made by both companies and individuals employed by the organisation will often include job advertisements. Employers can also advertise jobs on the sites. In the summer of 2015 Argos advertised on Facebook to attract Christmas temps by posting pictures of snowmen.

A key advantage for many employers using social media advertising is that they can advertise to and pinpoint precisely the audience they want to attract. Facebook allows companies to target their advertising by:

- Sex
- Age
- Interests
- Educational level
- Company
- Almost anything…

This facility is particularly useful to graduate recruiters, targeting job adverts by university or even degree, to recruit for graduate entry schemes.

So, if opening an account, don't just upload the most basic of information, but also think about what you place online as this additional information can help attract employers to your profile.

Candidate screening by employers

UK and US studies highlight extensive usage of social media in the recruitment screening process. A US study by Grasz (2015) highlighted how companies used social media in the recruitment process, recruiters particularly looking for positive and negative behaviour.

48% of users of social media had not employed a candidate because of what they found on social media, this included:

- Provocative / inappropriate photos
- Drinking or drug use comments
- Inappropriate blogs / Tweets
- Negative comments on employers
- People had lied about qualifications
- Discriminatory comments
- Career direction on social media indicating a desire to follow a different career direction to role applied for
- People had lied on a CV
- They had gained a negative feeling on the individual
- Poor communication skills – spelling or grammatical errors

But in the same way it can put an employer off, 75% of those using social media in the recruitment process said it supported their decision to interview a candidate. Information they found:

- Projected a professional image
- Helped fill in gaps on a CV
- Indicated good communication skills
- Good employer comments
- Supported qualifications
- Recommendations on their ability by others

So, if already active on social media, what do you have online? Try googling yourself to see what appears.

How to optimise your social media profile

Think about using social media to enhance your employment prospects. To help employment prospects for some it might mean they need to:

- Remove inappropriate material
- Close accounts
- Upgrade security to stop open access to information that might project a negative image

On the other hand, your positive image can also be enhanced by adding to information in social media such:

- Adding positive comments about your ability
- Adding comments about your skills
- Including your achievements on sites such as LinkedIn
- Undertaking networking activity to increase your professional image such as joining groups on LinkedIn and adding appropriate comments to discussions
- Obtain recommendations from ex-bosses to include on LinkedIn but remember not to recommend them back as this will undermine their validity - 'I'll rub your back if you rub mine'

Main social media platforms

Main social media platforms used or referenced in the recruitment process tend to be:

- LinkedIn
- Facebook
- Twitter

But there are also:

Google+, YouTube, Flickr, Pinterest, Instagram, Vimeo (creative people), + many others

Having already looked at LinkedIn, we are going to focus on Facebook and Twitter as there are the other two most widely reference by employers.

Facebook

Facebook is often referenced by employers when screening candidates as stated before so use it to promote yourself but when doing so:

- Keep friendly the information you place on there
- Try not to be too obvious when promoting yourself
- Use the same photo as on LinkedIn
- Watch spelling and punctuation

Recruiters may also use it as a CV database to contact candidates. Searching for example: "Engineers who work at Ford" will result in the recruiter finding in their results conversations / posts / updates / profiles of people with those key words in their Facebook profiles – mainly engineers who have or do work at Ford.

You can also search for vacancies yourself within an employer of choice. By searching "Jobs at Argos" you will see in posts and conversations Argos advertising jobs.

Google+

Although most people are on Facebook, Google introduced their own version Google+ several years ago, and it may also be worth creating a free account there to mirror your Facebook one. After all you don't know which employers are using which site.

Twitter

We hear a lot in the press about inappropriate Tweets, and employers are often looking at your Twitter account for this negative information. They do not want to employ a person who could pull down their reputation or damage their professional standing.

By posting your own Tweets or commenting on other Tweets you can enhance your professional image OR destroy it…! So, review your activity on Twitter well.

As mentioned previously, another use of Twitter is to follow an employer of choice – a company you would like to work for. By following a company, you will receive updates on vacancies as they are advertised.

Other factors to consider

When to apply for the job

The obvious answer to this question is as soon as you see it advertised, but let us go back to the comments made in the section 'Recruiters' CV alerts'. By uploading your CV on a Sunday, your CV will appear at the top of a recruiter's inbox; our comment implied it would be read first before older emails because most people read their email from the top down. However, some people do work from the bottom upwards.

So, if you see a job advertised at 7.00pm, should you apply for it at 7.00pm or wait until 7.00am the next morning? If the recruiter logs in later in the evening, your CV will be one of the first to be viewed – the same applies if they read their email bottom-upwards. If they log in first thing in the morning, your application could be at the bottom of the inbox, so there is no right or wrong answer.

Therefore, you might want to apply twice if you find an ideal role – once at 7.00pm and again at 7.00am, stating in your second application that you were not sure if your first application had been received, so you are sending it again to be sure.

The comment we started with was to apply for a job 'as soon as you see it advertised'. This is critical because many employers take jobs down within days or even hours after receiving sufficient numbers of applications. Even roles with closing dates often state nowadays that they may close off applications before the date stated if sufficient numbers of applications are received.

Following up applications

If you are applying for a job advertised by a recruitment agency, we recommend that you always ring them to check they have received your CV and looked at it.

When applying directly to a company, you can also follow up on your application but this can be far less productive.
If you do decide to follow up your application with a telephone call and get through to the relevant person:

- Introduce yourself and identify that you have applied for the role of ....
- Ask (if you do not already know) whether they have received your CV
- Try to quickly gain their interest by highlighting the skills you have that match their job requirements
- You could also ask
    o Is there any more information they need from you at this time?
    o Looking at my CV, do you feel my background and experience is right for this role?
    o Are there any other skills or experience you are looking for?
    o Even ask if you have an interview

By following up your application, you can often fill in the gaps and possibly provide supporting information to achieve an interview.

<u>Track and record your activity</u>

It is important to keep records and follow up on your activity. Vital information you need to record and track includes:
- Which job adverts you have sent your CV to
- Which companies you have sent your CV to
- Whom the CV was addressed to
- When it was sent
- When you need to follow-up your application
- In addition, you will need to remind yourself to:
  - Contact recruitment agencies at least every 2 weeks
  - Update your CV on CV databases weekly
  - Resend speculative approaches every 12 weeks
  - Resend your CV to recruitment agencies if not registering in person at least every 12 weeks

Remember to also keep a copy of the job advert and the exact CV you sent for the job. The CV may need to be tailored to individual job applications and you need to know what you may have changed.

You will also find that the adverts drop off the websites as the employers move towards interview. Job adverts also provide hints as to potential interview questions, so it is imperative you keep a copy of the original advertisement.

Covering letters

It is important to ALWAYS include a covering letter or email with an application. Line managers like to read them and, if used well, they can have a strong impact.

It is also CRITICAL that you do not simply use a standard copy and paste note, but instead one that highlights why your skills and experience are right for their job.

Although we are about to show you how to send a focused, short and to-the-point covering letter when applying for a job, you may need to send a longer covering letter when applying for some job roles.

Long covering letters

When a job advertisement highlights that you need to send your CV and a covering letter stating why you are right for the role, think 'application form'.

Many companies who used to use application forms in order to increase the diversity of applications have introduced a policy of allowing CV applications. As it can take several hours to effectively complete an application form, many people who were used to sending CVs tended to not apply for these roles because of the form. The employer still wants those people to apply and thus they now accept CVs, but the part of the application form they want to keep is the supporting statement where the applicant highlights specific experience. This means they ask for a covering letter to go with the CV in which you highlight your suitability for a role.

As with application forms where the supporting evidence box often states 'use additional sheets as required', they are expecting a detailed and comprehensive letter highlighting your suitability. This means your covering letter may include several pages of information where you provide precise and miniscule detail as to your suitability for a role. Ideally, then, start by providing top-level details, then specific details, then STAR-based examples (see the 'Completing application forms' section covered earlier).

Short, focused covering letters

For most applications we suggest a short and to-the-point covering letter. Producing these is relatively simple.

Start by tailoring your CV headline and bullet points. An example is below:

Experienced Warehouse Operative / Fork Lift Truck Driver

- **10 years' experience including Goods-In, Order Picking & Packing**
- **FLT Reach & Counter Balance Licences – loading and unloading lorries along with placing stock into the high racking**
- **Qualified First Aid Certificate and Fire Marshall**
- **Good IT Skills, including Word, Excel and bespoke IT Systems**
- **Excellent team player, self-motivated and quick to learn**

Next, simply copy this tailored CV heading into the template below and re-arrange the text into sentences.

Dear xxxx

I would like to apply for the vacancy of XXXXX XXXXXX as advertised on XXXXX. As you will see from my CV:
PASTE HERE CV Headline
If you require further information, please feel free to contact me on my mobile 07973 XXXXXX

Yours sincerely

Mr Edward Evans

Thus producing:

Dear Mr James

I would like to apply for the vacancy of XXXXX XXXXXX as advertised on Monster. As you will see from my CV:

I have a strong background in warehousing with over 10 years' experience. Areas I have worked in included goods-in, order picking, packing and general housekeeping.

I have also for the last 3 years operated Fork Lift Trucks and currently have Reach & Counter Balance Licences having loaded and unloaded Lorries along with placing stock into the high racking.

For the last 5 years I have been a qualified First Aider and Fire Marshall, and believe I have very good IT skills, being able to use Microsoft Word, Excel and bespoke IT Systems.

In all my previous roles I have been a strong contributor to my team, and see myself as self-motivated and quick to learn.

If you require further information, please feel free to contact me on my mobile 07973 XXXXXX

Yours sincerely

Even if you are not using our CV technique, note that the above covering letter highlights both experience and the soft skills the role requires. When writing your covering letter, regard the job advertisement the exam question, with the covering letter identifying your suitability for the role.

Action plans

Drawing from all the advice thus far, we advise you to complete an overview of activity – an Action Plan. We include both UK and Ireland action plans highlighting regional activity.

Action Plan – UK

Suggested CV Master Versions: Do you need several focused CVs? List:
(Remember to include generic job titles)

Remember to tailor your CV to individual job requirements   **Yes**

Carry out a Google / Bing / Yahoo search	
Search for Industry-Specific Job Boards **Search for Regional Job Boards** **Upload a CV to each site**	**List boards:**

Add you CV to these online CV databases

www.monster.co.uk	www.cv-library.co.uk
www.totaljobs.co.uk	www.fish4jobs.co.uk
www.jobsite.co.uk	www.reed.co.uk
www.indeed.co.uk	Plus others you find

Remember to refresh CVs on databases   **Weekly**   **Yes, without fail...!**

Set up 'Job Alerts' on:

www.indeed.co.uk	(Remember – Use the Advanced Search)
www.linkedin.co.uk	

Register with Recruitment Agencies	**List Agencies**

	Started Y / N	No of contacts
Networking		
Speculative Approaches		

Create a LinkedIn profile – include the phrase: 'Seeking new opportunity'

Action Plan – Republic of Ireland

Suggested CV Master Versions: Do you need several focused CVs? List:
(remember to include generic job titles)

Remember to tailor your CV to individual job requirements   **Yes**

Carry out a Google / Bing search	
Search for Industry-Specific Job Boards & Regional Job Boards	**List boards:**
Upload a CV to each site	

Add you CV to these online CV databases

www.monster.ie	www.indeed.ie
www.jobs.ie	www.cv-library.co.uk
www.irishjobs.ie	**Plus others you find**

Remember to refresh CVs on databases   **Weekly**   **Yes, without fail...!**

Set up 'Job Alerts' on:

www.indeed.ie	**(Remember – Use the Advanced Search)**
www.linkedin.com	

Register with Recruitment Agencies	**Yes**	**List Agencies**

	Started Y / N	**No of contacts**
Networking		
Speculative Approaches		

Create a LinkedIn profile – include the phrase: 'Seeking new opportunity'

Extra help and support

If you are struggling or feel you would benefit from extra help in areas such as CV writing, completing application forms, preparing for an interview, preparing for a presentation, preparing for an assessment centre or effective job hunting, we provide both remote support (via Skype and telephone) and individual face-to-face support.

Remote (Skype) support is purchased by the hour and available in the UK, Ireland and internationally.

Face-to-face support is provided on a 1-2-1 basis (UK and Republic of Ireland only)

For more information, please visit: www.job-doctor.com
Or email us at: info@job-doctor.com

Disclaimer

To the full extent permissible by law, Job Doctor disclaims all responsibility for any damages or losses (including, without limitation, financial loss, damages for loss in business projects, loss of profit or other consequential losses) arising in contract, tort or otherwise from the use of this guide, or from any action or decision taken as a result of using information and advice contained within the guide.

If any of these terms should be determined to be illegal, invalid or otherwise unenforceable by reason of the laws of any state or country in which these terms are intended to be effective, then to the extent and within the jurisdiction in which that term is illegal, invalid or enforceable, it shall be severed and deleted from the clause concerned and the remaining terms and conditions shall survive, remain in full force and effect and continue to be binding and enforceable.

These Terms and Conditions shall be governed by and construed in accordance with English law. Disclaimer issued – 6th April 2015.

Other Publications

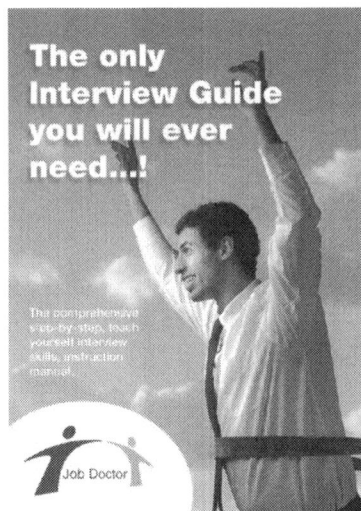

The only Interview Guide you will ever need...!

Printed in Great Britain
by Amazon